The Ultimate Guide To Overcome Anger

How To Manage Your Anger Before It Controls You

John K.

Table of Content

Check Out My Other Books

Introduction

A man of knowledge uses words with restraint, and a man of understanding is even-tempered.

-Proverbs 17:27

I want to thank you and congratulate you for purchasing the book, "The Ultimate Guide to overcome Anger".

This book contains proven steps and strategies on how to overcome anger.

This is an informative eBook which shall surely enlighten you in regards to ways of effectively curbing anger for an efficient lifestyle. The reader will get to know some of the probable situations that are more likely to trigger anger outbursts so as to avoid them. Various thoroughly researched inspiration ⬜uotes which are associated to standards of positive impetus books mainly in the field of anger management through mental control have been considered in the course of this ebook.

Also discussed are diverse principles and factors that are related to discovering the prime power which lies concealed within you once anger is kept under control. It is a fact that when you learn to control anger then communication issues and your ability to relate well with significant others will improve. As a result, you will have a healthy mental & psychological mindset for improved social functioning. Researchers have managed to prove that adequate meditation and leading a healthy lifestyle all play a major role in ensuring that one doesn't get stressed to the point of becoming angry. Uncontrolled anger outbursts will make one do very silly things that would later be regretted. For instance, some people have burned up their spouses due to very trivial issues. Only to later discover that this action disfigured them and would also necessitate lots of money in terms of hospital bills to cater for injuries sustained. Reading this script would aid one in knowing simple steps of controlling anger even in provoking situations.

This book has keenly delved into the extensive topic of attaining calmness through appropriate mind control techni ues. 'The Ultimate Guide to overcome Anger' is a step-by-step guide book that focuses on helping one to realize simple treasures of life that are hidden from those who regularly experience bouts of anger. These may for instance include inability of one to identify a potential wife and appropriately court for an established relationship leading to marriage.

You will also get to know ways in which one can effectively eliminate anger using appropriate humor. This therapeutic techni□ue against irritation does work for several ordinary cases in a person's life, plus it does help □uite a lot. Instead of getting nervous in regards to another individual's actions or behavioral trends one can decide to make amusement of the condition or words they are speaking. To relieve off stress that leads to tantrums one need to have the capacity to make fun out of negative instances. The person has to give appropriate explanations in regards to whatever has happened instead of laying blame on others and getting angry.

One can only get rid of anger using wit if he/she isn't a phobic towards terror and the situation isn't very grave. Your key purpose in anger management must always be in regards to avoiding any scuffle or fight even when another person offends you.

Thanks again for purchasing this book, I hope you enjoy it!

Chapter 1: An Overview of Humor as the Best Remedy for Combating Anger

Don't have anything to do with foolish and stupid arguments, because you know they produce quarrels.

-2 Timothy 2:23

You do not need to let anger to have control over you. Understanding following would help to overcome the anger.

Basic Life Skills to Avoid Temper Flares

This therapeutic techni☐ue works for many people and is one of the easiest to go by. When one requires you to fulfill an order which is too demanding for to bear with then it would be recommendable to give an ironic answer for such a confrontation instead of getting mad. For instance, you can make a rejoinder by asking whether the individual needs such absurd demands to be 'served from a dish.'

Another self help techni☐ue that would assist you in conquering anger outburst by learning how to sufficiently relax, along with accepting the situation as it is while taking care not to let temperatures flare.

Some conditions which are more likely to result in bursts of physical outrage are when the neighbor accidentally leaves trash just beside your doorstep. Instead of attacking the person with hands clenched it would be more reasonable to ask him/her about what led to such actions. Get to know the reason behind certain acts instead of just throwing tantrums.

When using humor, one should try to make fun out of negative circumstances. Try to validate what did happen like it was in reality preventing one from creating a relative much greater mistake. For example, if your parking spot was picked up by someone else it can be worthwhile to generalize that this is even better since the car could have been stolen were it not for the person picking up your spot.

Doing things on your own would also help a great deal in cooling down situations which could have otherwise turned out to be very severe. For instance, if the neighbor is indifferent by nature then one can decide to keep the surroundings clean on the person's behalf with a humorous mindset, instead of complaining and not changing the situation. When an issue has been solved then you should consider yourself as a great hero who is able to solve hitches that have been initiated with others devoid of quarrelling and only making matters worse than they ought to be. Doing something different once in a while would assist in helping you get to feel much better and avoid stressful situations that act as a seething pot for commencement of anger.

Give relevant explanations in regards to whatever did occur to you. Substantiate individual's behaviors or just make fun of whichever thing that's wrong and have a positive mindset that nothing would be able to eliminate your superior disposition or courage. It is only a fine-tuned positive mind frame that would effortlessly eradicate your emotional tempest and nervousness for whichever situation. If this is appropriately practiced then one would always be in a joyous mood and be in a position to live a convenient life and make wise decision devoid of anger bouts.

Being Angry but Still Keeping Cool

It would be a big lie for one to say that he/she doesn't get mad in the course of day to day life. As long as we were relating with others then they are bound to get in our nerves unintentionally. Remember that you also do the same without knowing. The best thing to do in such circumstances is staying cool and calm and trying as much as possible to control anger tantrums. Simply put, you need to learn how to control anger rather than letting it do the opposite.

- Take a quick deep breath. Immediately someone says or acts in a way that is supposedly offensive to you the best thing to do is breathing in sporadically. You will also need to wait for at least 10 seconds prior to taking any step. One needs to be still and sufficiently think through the matter before commencing with any course of action. This will take time & practice but will surely pay in the long run.

- Clarify the situation, then try as much as possible to explain circumstances in accordance to another individual's perspective, and not your own. This would help the offended person have a broader perspective on the issue than what was initially at his mind.

- You need to look at a provoking situation from three rather than two corners of a coin. Maybe the person who wronged you didn't intend to do so at first and it is you who had misunderstood this individual's actions. Shun the habit of repeatedly thinking only about yourself as in some cases you may be the one that's wrong. Many offences are simple misunderstandings that one can get well through when time is taken out to understand the situation in-depth.

- Keep a composed voice and considerable tone that will not make it clear to others that you are angry. When one is angry more often than not it will show with the individual's tonal inclination. Afterwards yells would follow and the person would start saying thing which they didn't mean at first. It is not appropriate for one to lash out whatever words which come to the mouth then think that later he/she would apologize to the offended person and expect to be forgiven instantaneously.

- If worse comes to worse just walk away since it is the easiest and most effective way to avoid a conflict. It is better to vent anger all on your own rather than including another person and making matters blow well out of proportion. When you are far from the offender you can proceed to yell the loudest, scream or even talk by yourself so as to vent out excess steam. Once you feel calm again is when you can now take the courage to face the offender Anger is an emotion and as we all know in many cases emotions generally make us not make rational decisions at pressing circumstances. Always try not to actively 'look' for definite reasons why you should be angry at the supposed offender since you will most definitely find them as they are already in your mind. Don't blow away stresses buy creating up tension with innocent individuals who are by no means related to the issues you have with the offender. Doing so will get you in trouble with them as well even if this was not your plan. Find improved ways in which you can sufficiently do away with stress without getting into the nerves of others. Remember that angry words do have the capacity of ruining up relationships and you therefore need to be extra careful in regards to the choice of words which are used when despite your emotional status.

Cooling Down When Vexed

Sometimes people do stress themselves way too much and this only makes anger outbursts blow way out of proportion. At such instances the best thing that one should do is just trying to remain as calm & cool as is possible.

You can consider keeping yourself as busy as is possible to avoid instances where you will be thinking about the person who offended you. Anger management experts have pointed out that at times one of the best cures needed for effective healing is just keeping our minds occupied. You can take a brisk walk across the park, do some washing or read a book just to keep the mind sufficiently occupied. This will assist in keeping the mind far off from disturbing thoughts which are key culprits of anger.

Clamorous settings will only serve to rouse up your anger. The most favorable thing to do when in a disturbing mental state is finding yourself some ⬜uite room to settle up your thoughts. If you are in a noisy setting walk out and find somewhere ⬜uieter. Allocate yourself some time alone for several minutes and shut off the rest who may be getting into your nerves.

Understanding Diverse Ways of Expressing Anger in A Bid To Eliminate It

Anger is part & parcel of our everyday life but one should not allow it to take control. When left unchecked bouts of anger may destroy you own family unit, lifestyle and also work relations. Incase you have the tendency of easily being irritated over very minor issues it's vital that you sufficiently learn ways of curbing extreme emotions for your own good.

This adverse emotion can only be dealt with if the victim understands this emotion better. The very first step for you to do is identifying the diverse categories of anger that we are prone to and different ways in which these emotions can be expressed. Through recognizing ways of expressing such feelings one shall be extra cognizant in regards to situations that are more likely to cause anger outbursts and consequently prevent them.

- Behavioral vexation. This type of anger is tied to physical expressions whereby one tends to act physically when expressing discontentment. It's usually revealed through unwarranted trouble making as well as defiance tendencies. At times there may be a desire to attack the subject which has caused these infuriated feelings in a bid to feel.

- Verbal anger. This kind of anger is usually delivered devoid of any physical action; it is expressed through word of mouth. The supposedly offended person will hurl belittling comments towards the other person along with hurtful criticisms. This will also include yelling profanity, blatant swearing or criticizing the other individual's abilities. Verbal anger can be very destructive to those who are emotionally sensitive.

- Passive. Those who express their emotions in this format will not react to the other person's provoking actions even though they may be hurting on the inside. Passively angry persons will hold onto their fury, particularly because they do think that expressing vexation ☐uite wrong. They may also be too scared to openly utter these feelings. Even though passively vexed individuals don't display anger forthright they will do it in other ways like silent treatment, sarcastic remarks or malevolent undertones. Others will try to avoid the individual or situation that does create such feelings. These groups of people are extremely good when it comes to devising covert or unorthodox methods of expressing themselves without directly confronting the offender. They can also be ☐uite dangerous.

- Self inflicted vexation. In this category the offended person acts in an unusual way by channeling emotional constraints towards him or her self. For instance, when anger does arise in individuals with low esteem they would express it through being quite hard on their own selves. The person would view the circumstances as a conse☐uence of own actions even though this may not be the case as the other person may have intentionally provoked the victim. Self inflicted anger does combine two very lethal emotions namely abridged self-esteem and quick vexation. People suffering from self inflicted bouts of anger will do gross things to their bodies such as slitting apart the wrists or starving themselves amongst other things.

It's imperative that one should know the diverse ways of expressing anger to be in a better position to manage any issues that pertain to vexation. It doesn't matter how you express anger as all in all any form of it is harmful. The best thing to do is learning how to control bouts of vexation to avoid explosive situations. If one does have issues in regards to getting angry then its imperative to assess your irritation tendencies and what are their most likely triggers so as to find a way around them. Jot down the ways which you are more likely to express these undesirable feelings and conduct a Google search to find procedures that you can employ to bring out desirable outcomes.

Detailed Practical Steps for You to Consider

- Those who are prone to physical expression of anger can try counting figures repeatedly up to the point which they would feel relieve from the emotion. Another healthy means of letting off steam is through engaging in controlled exercises. One can go for a jog in the park, lift a couple of weights or even relax in a serene environment and breathe in some cool fresh air. Boxing is also an effective exercise that will sure work wonders in aiding you release off unnecessary stem. Anger management experts have noted that there's nothing as liberating as punching a bag for a couple of minutes to discharge all relative traces of irate feelings away from your mental system.

- Anger victims who are more prone to oral rampage can consider learning how to bite the tongue & prevent insulting words from coming out. Another method would be simply walking way to prevent the anger outbursts from reaching dangerous levels. A person can learn to utilize affirmative self talk in a bid to defuse negative statements which may want to shove out. Try to convince yourself that the hurt feelings are there due to your own self being worked up and has nothing in regards to person who is supposedly the cause of these troubles.

- If you are into the habit of expressing anger or discontentment in sly or underhanded methods then it would be recommendable to try more direct but less harmful ways of expressing the emotion. But one needs to strike a balance not to be very direct since it's very possible to handle a situation without showing verbal or behavioral misappropriations. The main key for such instances is for one to be sufficiently assertive but not aggressive at all.

- Even more important is finding ways of building up a 'self-worth' mental state for those individuals who inflict injury upon themselves when they are vexed. Confidence and respect for personality are just some of the things you should work on in establishing a considerably healthy esteem that will help you not inflict injury on your body when mad.

- In cases like these one can try to have positive self-conversation sessions such as saying 'I'm a precious individual.' Reaping such words every day would definitely rise up your self esteem and assist you from unnecessarily getting angry on yourself.

All these anger control techniques would work differently depending on level of temperance and personality of the affected individual.

Chapter 2: An Overview of Practical Anger Management Techniques for Children

A patient man has great understanding, but a quick-tempered man displays folly.

-Proverbs 14:29

In the previous chapters we have learnt about some few applicable skills in regards to managing anger on your own. You now have ample knowledge in regards to the different ways one can express anger bouts and special techniques to counter these feelings. In chapter 2 we are going to discuss the following topics:

How parents can assist their children deal with emotional constraints.

Believe it or not kids can be very dangerous when they get angry and this is not only to themselves but significant others in their lives. This is particularly so due to the fact that they may be unaware of this feeling or when it does arise.

The causes of anger in adults are quite different from conditions that may lead to the same in young people. Grown ups usually express anger emotional disturbances through a blend of aggravation & key depressive disorder. On the other hand, children express vexation on simple material restraints such as taut clothing, toilet coaching or compulsion towards food.

• The parent needs to avoid placing pointless commands or using derogatory remarks which can arouse anger. These should never be dangled to the young person as they may be taken negatively. Provocative words are typically considered by the kids as directive mistreatment. These would then lead to feelings off depression, mild delusions, anger and also anxiety bouts.

• Parents also need to avoid the common habit of denying almost everything that their kids need further clarification on. Instead of this, the individual can provide workable alternatives to deal with situations as they arise. Kid's are not silly and would know when one is lying or saying the truth. In many cases they do develop anxiety tendencies when parents do show little concern about them or are too criticizing in regards to their actions.

• Averting or cutting down on provocation instances can also work wonders for your system. Remember that children are yet to learn and some of the behaviors they do engage in are done out of innocence. Being too harsh on them isn't wise as they can take your actions to mean a dislike towards them, and they will consequently act insensitively towards others.

• Avoid over-generalizing and highlighting one mistake over and over again. This would be seen as directional attack on them rather than trying to help them see their mistakes. Strive to be a parent who deals with issues forthrightly and at once rather than one who refers to mistakes that were done long ago and the kid has even forgot about them. Some actions can be irritating to respective parents and as destructive in relation to their personal welfare. These behavioral trends alone should never be entirely accounted in relation to thwarting or infuriating each activity the kid engages in. Talking matters out with them is a better alternative to yelling or labeling. It would definitely be very consoling to kids if their elders do share the good or awful feelings alike with them. The kid needs to be given suitable anger administration techniques to help them sufficiently express rage bouts in more constructive ways rather than destructive.

• In addition, parents also need to be good role models in regards to management of their own anger issues. Children will follow how their parents handle confrontational situations and would act in like manner while dealing with other individuals who may provoke them. Molding the little ones positively in relation to their uni ue expectations is a worthwhile art execution expressed by being a worthy model to follow.

• It's very safe to raise a kid in relation to a blossoming bud that is bound to give desirable habits. As a wise parent one should be conversant with several anger management strategies that can be applied to deal with confrontations as they emerge.

Anger! A Paradox of Emotions You Need Control

Many mental medics refer to anger as an absurdity that can make one do very gross mistakes if not dealt with promptly. Except for ardent saints we are all bound to become angry at one point or another in our lives. Anger results due to real or perceived prejudice or grievance, one does it to feel not only manly but also justified of what the other individual supposedly did. As human beings we feel satisfied retaliating as opposed to turning the other check as ethics dictates. Those prone to throwing anger tantrum s claim that it is much better to sufficiently express anger as opposed to bottling them up.

This adverse emotion can be comparable to an atomic bomb in the sense that it's radioactive in nature. When one is angry he/she would tend to act in ways that would also provoke others who are around. Vexation has the potential of damaging otherwise responsive relationships and can last for several successive years.

To know the full effects of uncontrolled anger think about the many battered wives as well as abused kids who are in the society, all this can be attributed to people who haven't been differentiated enough to know when not to cross the line.

In the American society violence related to anger has become very popular to the point that those engaged in such practices are said to be 'going postal' which is a term used to portray those with outbursts of irrepressible rage.

Many psychiatrists see anger as a subpart of several conditions rather than being a quandary on its own. In fact version III of the Diagnostic & Statistical Manual does have a standard class known as 'Intermittent volatile Disorder.' However, this clause was removed in the fourth version since it was not used by practitioners.

Incase ADHD(Attention deficit hyperactivity disorder) is also there then the combination would become even more detrimental. Anger isn't expressly a division of ADHD, though numerous traits in regards to the same will contribute towards triggering rueful circumstances.

Vexation does start with simple perception of injurious situations that are more likely to cause diverse impulses in relation to defending oneself antagonistically through attacking the offender. When someone suffers from ADHD, several perceptions are recurrently faulty since the itinerant attention structure does miss vital information which the active mind shall proceed to fill with pre-conceived faulty perceptions of self or the world at large.

This perceived affront will create shame and shut down ones capacity to appropriately analyze circumstances or inhibit the volatile rejoinder. The impulsiveness will trigger either fight or flight reaction, the latter being more common in those who are not used to direct confrontation when faced with dilemma.

Since anger doer feel appropriate and correct to those who practice it one may not feel or understand the impact as it is until when they have cooled down and witness its undesirable results.

There is an example where a man used to behave in a hostile manner towards his wife and it was not after the wife showed him a video of how he behave when in one of those negative moods that the dude felt pinched and realized why the wife wanted to leave him. This man apologized by saying he had no clue to what he was doing and that his desire was never to behave in like manner ever again.

5 basic steps that would assist you deal with anger

- Always find an excuse to walk away from confrontational situations. Fake a call, visit the nearby toilet or just stroll out of the place.

- Easily irritated parents who repeatedly get angry with their kids can learn to practice substitute parenting skills other than yelling &

throwing tantrums at the seemingly innocent kids.

- If things get tough then consider registering with an anger control program where you will learn more on yoga and deep meditation strategies.

- Psychological therapy especially in regards to behavioral strategies will assist one to comprehend the kin & cultural background as related to multigenerational transmission of anger tendencies. In some cases angry people can trace their behaviors to ancestral lineage of fore parents who also learnt to express their undesirable traits in like manner. Once this is identified the individual would be better positioned to know where to start from when faced with dilemma.

- The individual would pinpoint triggers which cause rage in addition to means of controlling such reactions.

Dealing with toddler tantrums

One fact about all toddlers is that they are highly sensitive and would scream, yell or throw tantrums at even the slightest provocations. As a parent you need to know how to cool them down so that they can not cause embarrassment in social settings. One effective method is practicing appropriate affection parenting techni ues. Toddlers who are regularly held close by their mothers do get perceptively responded to. They are extra calm, relaxed and would not throw unnecessary anger outbursts. Attached parents do read their kid's cues in a bid to logically create certain conditions that would drastically minimize chances of emotional outbursts. Kids lucky enough to have attached parents generally recover at a faster pace when faced with anger bouts than those who are raised in emotionally detached settings.   However, the parent should take care not to be over involved with the kid as this can result to cases of overdependence syndrome when the person finally grows up.

Another common techni ue is getting to identify triggers of such anger outburst and working through them to find stable solutions. A young kid is prone to tantrums in the event that they require something which they can't have or conse uently when you're occupied or are preoccupied with something extra.

You can restrain the behavior prior to its commencement by seeing it wholesomely and dealing with the same before it does escalate to irrelative heights.

When the toddler begins to whine and repeatedly grumble this can be a good indication that some action needs to be taken expeditiously. Your very first step should be trying to readdress and placate the kid before he/she does become even more upset about the circumstances. You can take the initiative of recording all the likely triggers that cause discomfort to your kid and ways you can positively ride through such situations with ease. The parent also needs to know when to strike the balance between helping a kid and when to let the child find his/her own way so as to know basic techni ues of surviving in this competitive world. Mothers should also consider extensive breast-feeding as a sure means of calming down toddlers who like to yell a lot. Afterwards, a short directed nursing session would work out well in further eliminating any traces of anger that may have remained.

The child can be taught on procedures of verbalization and trying out appropriate holding up therapeutic techni ues. In some cases all you need to do is just ignoring the child's tantrum fits. Refrain from getting forceful or swinging around with anger tendencies that your kid would be quick to learn. One effective way of taming irrelevant tantrums is ignoring them as much as possible, not unless the kid is facing real pain or is under duress. Remember that with toddlers tantrums are fed even more when one repeatedly responds to the child's flares. Children are attention seekers and in most cases they do throw feats just so you know that they are present. In many such situational confrontations wills have the propensity of elevating unconstructive behaviors. The individual has to know how to choose battles in a constructive manner and at the same time remember not to sweat up over minor stuff. A responsible adult should know when it's appropriate to walk away and ignore irrational behavioral trends to send a message to the infant that what he/she is doing isn't conventional to say the least.

Also have in mind that the young one is sufficiently growing at a fast pace and by now they may be in a position to verbally communicate. This simply means that the tantrum being thrown may be piled up frustration that the kid may wish to disclose to those around due to not being understood. One should endeavor to be considerate in regards to the kid's language systems. Help the young one get versant with basic skills necessary to understand gesticulation communication dynamics incase they don't know how to express themselves verbally.

Hormonal responses may also be responsible for tantrums in young people. Biologically, they can be considered to be responding to particular anguish and may not be in a position to efficiently control certain tantrums without sufficient help from those who are more experienced. This means the kid may be expecting to receive something but when its denied then this can be e□uated to a loss which will cause the young one's brain to trigger chemicals linked to pain, this is what would make the kid to be angry and throw feats. They anticipate something and if that is denied a tantrum could ensue. Denial equates loss and pain in the toddler's brain.

Remember that children are still young and it could be very difficult of them to appropriately distinguish difference between needs & wants as this is an elevated level of mind functioning which they may not be possessing. At such instances is when all the necessary parenting skills do play a big role. Some of these may include consoling, appropriate care giving, holding and being considerably close to them, along with responding in a positive manner. Such techniques will work towards calming down nerves through releasing brain hormones which serve this particular purpose. The child's 'love hormones' would instantaneously assist in soothing as well as erasing any traces of tantrum that the kid may be having.

Even when the parent has to leave the child in the hands of another care giver, the vital discussed techniques would still be very useful if applied well. Ensure that the care giver is responsive to the child's needs and is also friendly so that the kid can feel free to express feelings. One needs to be considerably clear in giving directions in regard to how the child needs to be treated by the caregiver.

Chapter 3:An Overview of Reducing Tantrum and Anger Amongst Adolecents

A quick-tempered man does foolish things, and a crafty man is hated.

-Proverbs 14:17

In the previous chapter we have learnt a few techni ues on how to deal with children and toddlers who express anger through throwing tantrums. We have seen that one of the most effective ways to address such issues is by showing affection to the kid and being responsive to genuine needs. Here, our focus would be ways one can use to address unwarranted stress, depression and anger amongst teenagers.

Adolescence is a very tumultuous stage in a person's life. It is a period where one does experience emotional upsurges that can lead to anger outbursts. Teenage is a intermediary phase of physical and intellectual human development which does take place amid childhood & maturity. The several changes which do occur can often cause confusion or mixed up feelings including unwarranted anger.

Even though this is just a typical human sentiment; teenage fury if not sufficiently controlled can result to rage mismanagement alongside other reactions which may be way out of standard proportions.

Indicators of adolescent fury outbursts to look out for

- If the young person does get furious at trivial issues such as what they want but can't get, or are inconvenienced by others in negative ways then its recommendable to render some anger management assistance.

- Incase the adolescent's anger causes him/her to act out aggressively through yelling, deliberately scheming for revenge or hitting others then something needs to be done and fast.

- Also of considerable weight is when the teenage has great difficulty in regards to moving on after occurrence of stressful events. Normal anger should be a provisional emotion but trouble only sets in when it exceeds the usual time frame.

- There are general things which do make most of us angry. However a troubled kid would become angry over issues that were initially managed sufficiently. The victim would pile up resentments over factors which at first didn't arouse any feelings, and these factors would continue to pile up by the day if not addressed promptly.

- If vexation manifestations do turn out to be self-destructive akin to reckless driving, then suicidal attempts along with perilous recreational activities may soon ensue.

When it comes to manifestation of anger teenagers can be classified into various subcategories which the parent needs to know about.

- The 'fighter' is an individual who plainly fights back when confronted, this can either be physically or through verbal abuse.

- 'Flight' reactors are the ones who prefer to run away or withdraw away from bouts of anger. This behavior is usually manifested through withdrawal from those perceived to cause the pain, and such may even include friends or family depending on intensity of the confrontation.

- The pretender. This is a teenager who does pretend that everything is fine but soundlessly plots diverse revengeful acts. Such activities are regularly connected with quite devious behavioral trends and repeated lies.

Cooperative Management Tips

- Strive to distinguish the main reason behind such anger trends. Every action can be based upon some underlying factor whether legit or presumptuous. If it is due to worthy reasons then it would be meaningful for you as a parent to address these issues before they blow way out of proportion.

- Get to know several triggering points so that you can be better prepared to tackle factors and know from where to start from when dealing with the young ones anger issues. There are certain general issues which are prone to trigger the teen's anger. Through repeatedly taking key note of such characteristic causes, latent future hysterical fits can sufficiently be done away with.

- Talk things out. Responsible parents need to converse about diverse changes along with issues pertaining to the teen amongst several other factors that are within the family scope.

- Be fit. Constant exercise is simply an exceptional way of relieving off burdensome stress. An adolescent should be encouraged to do so in a bid to shed off all unnecessary stress.

Explaining Defiance and How It Is Linked to Anger

- Defiant disorders amongst teenagers can mainly be discussed in accordance to two major characteristics that include anger along with opposition. Antagonistic defiant disorder is the one which is less grave although its level of seriousness will vary depending on personality of the affected person. When left unchecked 'ODD'(Oppositional defiant disorder) would result to Conduct Disorder which is a graver condition.

- At times those who show signs of anger bouts when they are adolescents can trace such tendencies to childhood, particularly if one had been raised in a chaotic family setting. A troublesome, obstinate kid may be sufficiently diagnosed with the ODD(Oppositional defiant disorder) syndrome while still a toddler, though it's typically revealed later on when they reach adolescence. The trend can be characterized by certain unwarranted behaviors such as intentionally annoying others, rage tantrums, denial of obedience, continuous arguing & breaking of set rules, easy irritation and spitefulness, being unkind or blaming others when mistakes clearly rest on you. An adolescent with ODD(Oppositional defiant disorder) can be very manipulative and will more often try to make other family members incite and ꓷuarrel amongst themselves for mistakes that he/she instigated.

- Conduct disorder would be diagnosed in the event that a child does escalate relative anger conducts by including physical violence directed towards other innocent parties. Other things to look out for are property damage, petty theft, lying and mistreatment of family pets. Researchers have established two clear onsets in regards to anger A) Childhood onset.

This is where a verdict is made prior to the kid reaching the age of 10yrs; symptoms can begin to show up during the kindergarten years B) Adolescent onset. In such cases a diagnosis would be finalized after the individual has attained age 10 and above. However, the parent needs to remember that both of these are ☐uite hard to treat. But there's some green light in the latter version since here the affected person is fully aware of its existence and can therefore be helped with more ease.

- Researchers haven't been able to pinpoint the main causes of anger problems in kids. One principal school of reason holds on that such tantrums usually show up due to repressed negative emotions that one may be harboring. It's these feelings which later escalate to higher levels that show up more during adolescence. Proponents of this theory claim that such resentments usually occur when the kid is 'fixated' or not able to pass through some basic developmental stages. The other common theory assumes that unconstructive behavioral trends usually occur as an effect to unfitting family settings; particularly where the child is reared within an inconsistent, excessively punitive and judgmental parenting setting.

- In most cases ODD will be sided alongside CD especially when symptoms are correlated. Professionals have rated such effects on a pedestal of around 65%. Mood disorders including depression, bipolar effects and also anxiety are also ◻uite common. In rare cases learning dysfunctions would also be present in teenagers with excessive anger because their ability to concentrate would greatly be hindered. A kid that is showing trouble in regards to learning or getting the mind fixed on certain topics would most likely become frustrated due to lack of comprehension in relation to concepts that other kids find very straightforward. This will further feed up the already aggravated tempers to heights that can be detrimental. Such adolescents would be depressed, over anxious, frustrated and will tend to act out even in situations that don't warrant any emotional outbursts.

- There are numerous outcomes that may be related to the child suffering from ODD. Nearly half of all kids who get diagnosed with the condition get out of the negative tantrum habit by the time they are about 8yrs old. But 5-10% of this population would have diagnosis altered in the course of life top become ADHD. A kid will hence continue having ODD and no other symptom even though this can seem unusual to the parent. Another set of kids may escalate such behaviors and they will further be clinically diagnosed with Demeanor Disorder. Lastly, some kids will develop additional problems apart from the conventional ODD.

- It's important to look into underlying factors that contribute to the kid's defiance tendencies rather than generalizing issues and discriminating the adolescent without understanding. Treatment would definitely be much simpler when one has a very clear picture in regards to all relative contributing factors.

- The most result-oriented treatment in regards to controlling anger amongst teenagers should be channeled and better parenting techniues. In most cases 'Parental Managing Tutorship' also abbreviated as 'PMT' is the system used to encourage most parents into focusing on the positive behavioral tendencies of the adolescent through reward & reinforcement while punishing or applying sanctions on those that are deemed negative. The trainee would also be trained on how to sufficiently ignore negative behavior in a way that the child's ego would not be fed.

- While medication can be a ꟸuick fix when dealing with anger many parents prefer taking their children to boarding program facilities that are specially equipped to cater for kids with depressive and aggressive tendencies. When it comes to anger management it's vital to commence treatment as soon as symptoms begin to show up. This is so because ODD tends to escalate in intensity the more it is left untreated.

- The steady succession of childhood CD is reasonably predictable and the parent can stem it before escalating to unwarranted and explosive levels. Angry adolescents regularly indulge in risky behaviors to let off steam. These can include drug abuse, perilous sexual conduct, and unlawful gang activities. When left untreated for long rage can lead to other detrimental disorders such as depression & 'Antisocial Behavioral Disorder.' Many kids who do have anger bouts may be ignorant of their origins and therefore need proper directions from adults so that they can grow up to become law-abiding and responsible grownups.

Chapter 4: An Overview of How the Working Class Population Can Manage Their Anger Problems

A hot-tempered man must pay the penalty; if you rescue him, you will have to do it again.

-Proverbs 19:19

In the previous chapters we have learnt about different ways one can successfully deal with tantrum issues in toddlers and also the teenage age group. Here, our main focus would be ways in which busy official persons can improve their chances of managing anger so as to improve their repute at work.

Things to Consider While Formulating Reasonable Goals to Deal With Anger Issues

The very first step for successful anger management is studying your lifestyle to know the things which are more likely to cause you emotional turmoil in the work place. After identifying this proceed to rank these factors depending on their level of intensity so that you can know which ones to deal with first and those that can wait for later.

- First you have to efficiently make it ꓘuite clear what your needs would be. When this is done one needs to be cautious not to get over aggressive in regards to the set demands. If you become over insistent with such then most likely you shall meet even more opposition as cooperation from significant others.

- At many instances people only do care in regards to their own needs and nothing else. This isn't worthwhile since such reasoning can only lead to stress since you can get into other people's nerves while trying to fulfill your own selfish ambitions. To avoid getting angry with others in the office setting learn how to be calm & composed then consider the opinions of others as well since yours may not necessarily be the best, be someone who listens.

Goal and Respective Assistance

When you have formulated a clear goal at mind it is advisable to establish a directional blueprint that would explain the circumstance you are going to dealing with. Other stakeholders need to have solid reasons in regards to how they may assist you. For example, the gym expert would reꓘuire your BMI amongst other indexes to aid you work out in the correct manner to relive stress, anger & anxiety.

While relating with others in the work setting don't forget to be gracious at all times and also thankful in regards to the assistance which is offered to you. Both of these two things would aid you to set individuals in a proper mind frame in which they would be in a position to do whatever they ca within their power to see your success. Such factors will tremendously cut down on the levels of stress or depression and further boost your relationship with colleagues.

Learn How to Appropriately Relax

To manage anger with ease you need to know a few basic inhalation techni ues that have been proven to help people calm down irate nerves. When anger starts to show up you can take some break and gasp in short deep breaths in a rhythmic manner. But don't overstress yourself while doing this since frustration has also been know to emerge when one is trying very hard and stressing up.

It's true that you're working towards fulfillment of a worthy goal at work, but remember that reaching there in a single piece is much more important. There's only a limited amount of work which one can do within a day's time and once this is complete then the needs to rest. Frustration and unwarranted anger will set in when one tries to stuff that are beyond the body can take per given time period.

Take out some ☐uality time for sake of refreshment. You'll notice that others would consent into letting you put together some energetic steam such that when one commences work again set enthusiasm would push you forward instead of just having to pull through drearily.

Handling Complaints

In cases where one is to handle frustrations you should take heed to complain in such a way that will not upset the individuals who are assisting you. If you do condemn then the parties affected will definitely not offer their best in regards to sufficiently looking after your varied interests.

The person on treatment should always have a clear mind frame especially in regards to criticisms. Remember that harboring negative feelings concerning what others did say to you in the past would serve no good at all. If you allow your resentments to lead you towards annoying others then

9 out of 10 chances high that the aggravation would be thrown right back at you.

Anger is like a seething pot and the best way to tame it is by cutting off its supply. In this case 'supply' would refer to those conditions that are more likely to get you upset such as problems from outside the office setting or home which may include broken relationships or family wrangles.

Learn how to separate professional work from personal issues. When one does wrong you ensure that the matter is settled promptly between you before it turns out to be a grudge that would make all the parties involved including you angry for nothing.

Also remember that anger as well as frustration is reproduced and conveyed back towards the individual; who did instigate it at first. If all the other strategies do hit a dead end then it would be worthwhile to try out the anger control techniques. But you should note that these are not guaranteed systems and would only work depending efforts applied and your personality traits.

Chapter 5: An Overview of Dealing with Anger in the Office

In your anger do not sin; when you are on your beds, search your hearts and be silent

-Psalm 4:4

In chapter 4 we have learnt some few helpful tips in regards to how one can manage anger in the office setting through relating well with other colleagues. In this section we are going to focus on methods one can use to help the elderly sail through their unwarranted anger bouts.

There nothing as dangerous as when an old person gets vexed since several organs in his/her body would also be negatively affected. If anger levels are too high the loved one may develop a stroke or heart attack which may turn out to be lethal if not addressed promptly.

One of the most popular techni ues when addressing anger is identifying a peer group that is also interested in doing the same. Here the elderly will get to learn and share fury control skills with others for positive outcomes. So as to establish the anger control activities which would bear more fruits it's vital that one gets versant with activities that are more likely to trigger furious behavioral trends. Researchers have been able to distinguish four basic triggers of extreme anger in the elderly. Some of them have been discussed as follows:

- Biological origins. Those that are swift to convey vexation may be prone to exaggeratingly sharp instinctual responses that make them act out in aggressive ways.

- Life experience. This can generate an increased sum of triggers that pertain to aggression or frustration.

- Mistaken perception. Those who wrestle with anger bouts do assume certain things concerning the environment as well as stakeholders in their livers but in many cases such presumptions maybe untrue.

- Miscommunication. Anger may be seen as a swift but extreme reaction towards a circumstance which may be well resolved by means of diplomatic discussion. The main key is helping the elderly learn ways of conversing with others in a manner which isn't confrontational.

Identification

The key anger control activity would be actively identifying the commencement of anger bouts. While at the group counseling setting, a qualified moderator can request individuals to actively identify when they begin to feel angry. Moreover, the person would be asked to identify the person whom they are vexed with and deal with any latent grudges forthrightly instead of harboring them inside the heart.

The individual on treatment can respond through pinpointing another individual within the group whom these resentful feelings are channeled towards. These two individuals would agree to confer the remorse feelings without any kind of interruption from third parties or meaninglessly jumping into conclusions.

The key goal in such a therapeutic technique is voicing hurtful emotions and finding ways of resolving issues once and for all while leaving the vexation behind them. Striving towards resolution within a safe setting like group therapeutic counseling is a very effective anger control system.

Types

There are various categories of anger and also divergent anger control activities which can work best towards addressing them. Repressed anger can necessitate a severe physical action to let loose long-held aggravation.

Singing along to loud melody, striking a punching bag or leaping onto a trampoline can assist in doing away with unnecessary anger. Note that fresh anger can be attributed to an urgent response towards a contemporary circumstance.

The ideal action channeled for such kinds of vexation is concerned with sufficiently analyzing particular triggers and categorizing them in form of a series. One needs to jot down a sure list of such triggers and also learn definite ways of how to sufficiently deal with the same when they commence. This is before it reaches to the explosive stage. Do whatever it takes to effectively pass through particular trigger circumstances. Change the setting, envisage an optimistic notion or commence to take some sure deep breaths.

Effects You Should Expect As a Parent

One sure and ideal effect pertaining to fury management activities concerns a person who will not only get to discover self-soothing procedures but will further suffer lesser stints in relation to anger. Individuals can best accomplish such a feat with help from an experienced therapist or support grouping. Doing such allows individuals to sufficiently realize that they aren't on their own while undergoing suffering.

One would understand that many individuals do struggle with vexation and productively find activities which would aid in managing or alleviating such. Therapy also renders a formal setting for actual celebration of achieved goals in a communal setting. One would be able to celebrate a flourishing meeting of temporary goals directed towards alleviation of anger.

Warning

Anger control isn't a strategy that would work for all people in the same fashion. A chief predicament as concerns anger control activities is in the fact that they set individuals in a very tight or alien situation which by itself serves as a sure trigger. Individuals should identify a setting or situation that they are more comfortable with.

Then strive to challenge their expectations as of this point. Doing such means that the individual would ultimately become   more successful in regards to conveying anger management activities towards the sure real of actual life.

Wrapping up

Vexation is a natural sentiment which we regularly utilize in form of a survival mechanism and it comes to play when one is unable to satisfactorily articulate real meaning of sentiments that they have. It is regularly a secondary emotion which is experienced in a whole lot of ways. When individuals begin to sense enragement it's mainly as a result of primary feelings which they haven't taken considerable time to categorize.

Let's take into consideration a real life event of a man who flew a private jet right into an IRS building way back in 2009. There were numerous precipitating issues which instigated such an event to happen. This person wasn't able to sufficiently support his own family and had a fixed amount of income. Soon after the IRS did wipe out all that was in his savings account due to the fact that he had some outstanding debt. Despite the fact that this dude had all reasons to be angry it still doesn't justify how he reacted. He was undergoing several negative emotions which include hopelessness, defensive traits, inadequacy, stress and unwarranted worry. If this man did have skills along with coping mechanisms relevant in tackling such emotions before they turn disastrous then most probably he would still be living as per the moment, but it's sad to say that his own anger mismanagement led to eventual demise. Below are key tips that can assist one to appropriately manage anger:

- Clearly reflect upon respective thought processes in a definite self-talk system. At many times people do make large mountains in their brains from issues that are very trivial. In other words we do make situations exaggeratedly larger than what is happening in reality. The best way to deal with anger is to stifling it before it commences.

- Learn to be an effective listener. For proper communication to take place one needs to be a good listener because conversation is a two way process. At many instances we do react in ways that are plainly wrong since we may misunderstand the other person's statements. For one to listen well it is recommendable to keep the lips shut and do more of listening. It can be difficult to go by this if you're not used to it, but once you begin then chances are high you will get used to it.

- Evaluate the costs which would be incurred. This will help you know whether reacting would be beneficial or costly. Remember that there are several ways in which one can react rather than throwing tantrums. The simple message to consider is thinking prior to taking action.

But be careful because this shall not occur overnight. There isn't any quick fix to such issues since it would re□uire you to engage in considerable practice. But the more you do think about it you'll realize that it isn't hard at all. To avoid being a victim of temperature flares always learn how to practice deep meditation when faced with confrontation. This shall aid you identify weak spots that you should put more emphasis on in terms of practice so as to efficiently alleviate all anger issues.

Conclusion

Thank you again for purchasing this book!

I hope this book was able to help you to understand the issue with anger and provide the cure for it.

The next step is to take action on the steps mentioned in this ebook.

Finally, if you enjoyed this book, please take the time to share your thoughts and post a review on Amazon. It'd be greatly appreciated!

Thank you and good luck!

Check Out My Other Books

Below you'll find some of my other popular books that are popular on Amazon and Kindle as well. Simply click on the links below to check them out. Alternatively, you can visit my author page on Amazon to see other work done by me. If the links do not work, for whatever reason, you can simply search for these titles on the Amazon website to find them.

1) The Ultimate Guide To Become An Early Riser For Life - How To Awake Early And Be Productive Forever

Or go to: http://amzn.to/1MRDEMr

2) The Ultimate Guide To Become An Alpha Male - How To Attract Women, Win In Life And Be Confident

go to: http://amzn.to/20G8bB0

3) The Ultimate Guide To Overcome Porn Addiction For Life - The Most Effective, Permanent Solution To Finally Stop Porn Addiction

go to: http://amzn.to/1NZ2tmN

4) The Drug Addiction Cure - The Most Effective, Permanent Solution to Finally Overcome Drug Addiction for Life

go to: http://amzn.to/1kkb9uc

5) How to Stop Snoring for Life - The Most Effective Cures and Remedies for Snoring

go to: http://amzn.to/1NE9uLn

6) India - The Land of Mystery, Mysticism, Mythology, Miracles, Multiculturalism, and Mightiness

go to: http://amzn.to/1kkbBc5

7) The Ultimate Cures And Remedies For Hair Loss

go to: http://amzn.to/1M1xFRC

8) The Ultimate Guide To Overcome Rejection - How To Get Back To Life After A Rejection

go to: http://amzn.to/1M1xMMZ

9) The Ultimate Guide To Overcome Marijuana Addiction

go to: http://amzn.to/1M1xQMN

10) The Ultimate Guide To Overcoming Shopping Addiction - The Most Effective, Permanent Solution To Finally Control Compulsive Shopping and Buying Disorder

go to: http://amzn.to/1L60iJr

www.ingramcontent.com/pod-product-compliance
Lightning Source LLC
Chambersburg PA
CBHW050516290526
45786CB00007B/2584